D1038466

𝔓resented to ....

....

....

....

KATE GREENAWAY'S

BIRTHDAY BOOK

✲Kate·Greenaway's✲

Birthday·❀·Book

WITH 382 ILLUSTRATIONS,

DRAWN BY KATE GREENAWAY,

VERSES BY MRS. SALE BARKER.

Derrydale Books
New York

This edition is published by Derrydale Books,
a division of Crown Publishers, Inc.
    c d e f g h
DERRYDALE 1980 EDITION

Manufactured in the United States of America

Library of Congress Cataloging in Publication Data

Greenaway, Kate, 1846–1901.
    Kate Greenaway's Birthday book.

    Reprint of the 1880 ed. published by G. Routledge,
New York, under title: Kate Greenaway's Birthday book
for children.
    SUMMARY: Includes a blank space and a verse for
each day of the year.
    1. Greenaway, Kate, 1846–1901—Juvenile literature.
2. Birthday books—Illustrations—Juvenile literature.
3. Children's poetry, English. 4. Birthday books.
[1. Birthday books. 2. English poetry] I. Barker,
Lucy Davies, 1841– II. Title. III. Title: Birthday book.
NC978.5.G7A4   1980   741.64'2'0924   79-28520
ISBN 0-517-31005-8

FOREWORD

March 17 should be a special date in everyone's *Birth-day Book*, for it was on that day in 1846 that Kate Greenaway was born. Her beautifully illustrated books appeal to everyone who loves springtime, nature, and the freshness and innocence of childhood. The publication of this edition marks the one hundredth anniversary of its original publication in 1880 —added proof that Kate Greenaway's art is timeless in its universal appeal.

"I fear it is conceited," she said, "but there are a *very few* drawings—little ones of my own—that I do not get tired of . . .." The little drawings here—one for each day of the year, plus more—will delight and amuse you for as long as people have birthdays.

The equally delightful verses accompanying each picture were written by Mrs. Sale Barker. They inspired Robert Louis Stevenson to try his hand at some rhymes for children; the result was *A Child's Garden of Verses*.

With the continuing interest in astrology, many people associate their birthdays—perhaps unwillingly—with such creatures as crabs, bulls, or scorpions. How much more refreshing to remember your birthday (and your friends') with a dimpled doll dressed for a wintry walk, a stout little boy playing ball, "a beautiful Iris,/Soft purple," or "The two twin Master Twinklebys."

Twelve color plates, originally printed by the excellent artist Edmund Evans, treat us to a wonderful view of Kate Greenaway's brightly colored world. Pictures such as these inspired her very good friend John Ruskin to say:

> . . . Miss Greenaway, with a profound sentiment of love for children, puts the child alone on the scene, companions him in all his solitudes, and shows the infantine nature in all its naïveté, its gaucherie, its touching grace, its shy alarm, its discoveries, ravishments, embarrassments, and victories; the stumblings of it in wintry ways, the enchanted smiles of its spring-time, and all the history of its fond heart and guileless egoism.

CARY WILKINS

KATE GREENAWAY'S BIRTHDAY BOOK

JANUARY 1ST.

WHAT are the bells about? what do they say?
Ringing so sweetly for glad New-Year's Day;
Telling us all that Time never will wait,
Bidding us use it well, ere it's too late.

JANUARY 2ND.

A large brown muff, for cold, cold hands,
So dainty, too, trimmed up with bows;
Of all comforts the best, when you have
    to go out,
On a day when it freezes or blows.

5

JANUARY 3RD.

There was an old woman who shook,
The wind her umbrella it took;
    She cried, "The wind's strong,
    I can't hold it long;"
And that's why she trembled and shook.

JANUARY 4TH.

A great big muff and feathered hat,
    Poor little legs look bare;
A curious little figure this,
    Enough to make you stare.

JANUARY 5TH.

The joys of the tea-pot who will not sing?
The warmest and cosiest comforting thing!
Who does not enjoy a good cup of tea?
Without taste or reason I'm sure they must be.

JANUARY 6TH.

So bright, so fresh, so delightfully nice,
To skim along on the hard smooth ice !
What fun to fly on your skates away,
Skating so gaily the whole of the day !

JANUARY 7TH.

Old Mrs. Big-bonnet, little Miss Wee,
Out for an airing, as you may see ;
Chatter and chatter, and pleasantly talk,
Enjoying together their nice winter's walk.

JANUARY 8TH.

Who wouldn't go to a Fancy Ball ?
High-heeled shoes to make us tall ;
Ribbons, and laces, and powdered head,
And then to dance a minuet led.

7

JANUARY 9TH.

I've seen many Quakers, and Guys a few,
And I think this a frightful Guy—don't you?
Just look at her bonnet, and look at her back!
To dress herself well she hasn't the knack.

JANUARY 10TH.

A Turk with a hookah, I declare!
I think this will make you little ones stare.
Perhaps he's the Sultan, come over to see
If he in this Birthday Book will be.

JANUARY 11TH.

Dear little Baby! he's wrapped up so warm,
    And just beginning to run;
Out in the frosty day, roses to win,
    Fresh air, and plenty of fun.

8

JANUARY 12TH.

A jug and a basin—for what, do you think?
With water to wash little fingers from ink;
For some little children, alas! are so
Fond of touching such things, you know.

JANUARY 13TH.

Roly-Poly with a snowball,
Throwing it at nothing at all;
Roly-Poly round about,
It seems to me he's very stout.

JANUARY 14TH.

So wearied with her heavy load!
So ragged, sad, and cold!
Dear children, always pity show
To those who're poor and old.

9

JANUARY 15TH.

A clown, or a jester, I fancy this man,
But really I can't be sure, think as I can;
His hair stands on end, and his waist's very long,
And he looks just as if he was singing a song.

JANUARY 16TH.

A cottage so rustic, and pretty, and
    warm;
  Would you like to live in it, pray?
Little children, I dare say, are living
    there now,
  And, though poor, are happy all
    day.

JANUARY 17TH.

My dear little lady, now why turn your back?
  I am sure that your face is fair;
Yet we see but your dress, and the round of your
    cap,
  Not even a vestige of hair.

JANUARY 18TH.

If you have cows, here's something
    to feed them,
    Something most juicy and sweet ;
A fine mangold-wurzel is what cows
    delight in,
    To them 'tis a wonderful treat.

JANUARY 19TH.

Small black-haired child, with a chubby
    round face,
    Two little round eyes, and round nose ;
Little fat arms, and little white frock,
    And out peep the dear little toes !

JANUARY 20TH.

There was an old woman, whose hat
Was all peaked, and not at all flat ;
    On her back was a hump,
    That stuck out in a lump,—
'Twas a trouble to her when she sat.

JANUARY 21ST.

Of an empty chair, when it's ugly, too,
Why, what can we say, between me and you?
We only can fancy some lady fair
Is coming to sit in the empty chair.

JANUARY 22ND.

A very grand lady, come out for a walk,
   What a feather, and large-brimmed hat!
So very important, yet only a child,—
   We all very well can see that.

JANUARY 23RD.

Just see what a pace he is rushing along!
   Just look at his nose and his chin!
His hat, and his pig-tail, his curious legs,
   And his arms, too, so awkward and thin

JANUARY 24TH.

Pray, young lady, where are you going?—
　　Out for a winter's walk;
To breath fresh air, and come home fair,
　　And then some tea and talk?

JANUARY 25TH.

Useful and ornamental too,
　　Handsome in colour and form
Cream-jugs may peaceful and pleasant be,
　　Though tea-pots sometimes have a storm.

JANUARY 26TH.

Sitting by the fireside, thinking of the past,
Of the time, long faded now, far too bright to
　　last;
Waiting patiently and still, for the end to come,
Looking—with what wistful eyes!—for the last
　　long home.

13

JANUARY 27TH,

This woman is going to market,
  With a basket full of eggs ;
She has many a weary mile to walk,
  I pity her tired legs.

JANUARY 28TH.

Goosey, goosey, gander !
  With a night-cap on his head ;
He turns himself, and twists himself,
  And then he goes to bed.

JANUARY 29TH.

Footstool, or hassock, whichever you call it,
  Is useful enough in its way ;
But it helps little people sometimes to a tumble,
  And big people, too, I may say.

JANUARY 30TH.

What is he doing, this little Jack Horner;
   There on his three-legged stool?
Is he doing his lessons, or eating his dinner;
   Or merely just playing the fool?

JANUARY 31ST.

Baby is looking for father,
   He's been such a long time away;
Father is coming to baby,
   Has thought of her all through the day.

FEBRUARY 1ST.

Is this Queen Elizabeth, may I ask,
   With her ruff, and her cushioned head?
No, for this lady still proudly walks,
   And Queen Elizabeth's dead.

FEBRUARY 2ND.

Cabbages red, and cabbages green,
This is a fine one as ever was seen ;
Cabbages grow in the garden near,
Cabbages grow the whole of the year.

FEBRUARY 3RD.

This is Master Baby, paying a morning call,
Sitting so good upon his chair, but speaking not at all :
Listening to every word, the funny little man !
Wondering at the news he hears, thinking all he can.

FEBRUARY 4TH.

Hush-a-bye, Dolly ! go to your rest ;
    Mother wants to be busy, you know.
Dolly, be quiet, I won't have you cry ;
    To sleep, child, you really must go.

FEBRUARY 5TH.

A nice new broom, to sweep away,
    And keep the floor so clean;
The crumbs and dust all disappear,
    There's not one to be seen,

FEBRUARY 6TH.

The wind, determined to have some fun,
Blew an old woman to make her run;
The old woman trotted along with a will,
But stopped at last, when she got to a hill.

FEBRUARY 7TH.

A kite, one day, flew up in the sky,
    To try and reach the sun;
He failed, and he fell with a broken string,
    And sighed, "It can't be done!"

FEBRUARY 8TH.

There was an old person too fat,
Who wore a remarkable hat :
    He said, " Let the world talk,
    I 'll take a good walk,
And try to get rid of this fat."

FEBRUARY 9TH.

A shuttlecock was sent so high,
He very nearly reached the sky ;
When he came down he was so vain,
They never sent him up again.

FEBRUARY 10TH.

Little maid, little maid, whither away,
Running so fast on this early-spring day?
Perhaps it 's Mamma you are going to meet,
And Love lends his wings to your little feet.

FEBRUARY 11TH.

Turnips and carrots are all very fine,
If on boiled mutton you're going to
    dine;
But, as that is a dish that I really
    can't bear,
I 'll willingly give up to you all my
    share.

FEBRUARY 12TH.

A pot of spring flowers before me stands,
    Primroses fresh and fair;
Telling of days that are coming soon,
    When their sweetness fills the air.

FEBRUARY 13TH.

Carrying home the washing,
    Snowy-white and clean;
Merry maidens bring it home,
    As can well be seen.

19

FEBRUARY 14TH.

Pray, little lady, why do you come out,
　　When it's raining in this way?
Perhaps an important letter to post?—
　　I remember, it's Valentine's Day!

FEBRUARY 15TH.

Johnnie has got a new peg-top,
　　That spins with wonderful grace;
The boy is surprised and delighted,
　　Just look in his eager face.

FEBRUARY 16TH.

Polly, the milkmaid, comes over the plain,
　　Fills up her milk-pails, and then back again;
Milk for our breakfast, milk for our tea,
　　Thank the good moo-cows for you and for me.

FEBRUARY 17TH.

The old pump stands in the meadow,
  Where all the cows are fed, O !
To give them a drink is but fair, I think,
  So the old pump stands in the meadow.

FEBRUARY 18TH.

Little Laura Lazy lies against the wall ;
If she spends her time so, she 'll do no work
    at all.
Softly we will touch her, give a little shake,
Then, perhaps, this idle maid may think it
    time to wake.

FEBRUARY 19TH.

Little Tom Thumbkin blows bubbles so light,
Up they go—higher yet—colours so bright ;
Little Tom Thumbkin looks quite forlorn,
Why, do you think, it is?—bubbles are gone.

21

FEBRUARY 20TH.

An empty chair! an empty chair!
Come and sit down on it, any who dare:
It looks so firm, but give it a shake,
And into pieces it soon will break.

FEBRUARY 21ST.

"Little friend, little friend, why stare you so?"
"I'm looking, I'm looking, to see the wind blow."
"Little friend, little friend, have you a mind
To become a small pig? They alone see the wind."

FEBRUARY 22ND.

A good-sized bonnet, a very small dog,
As you can plainly see;
The bonnet would do for a kennel too,
It really seems to me.

FEBRUARY 23RD.

" Baker, what have you got in your basket
    Something good, I trust."
" Cakes and buns, jam tarts and biscuits,
    Pastry with nice thin crust."

FEBRUARY 24TH.

A Japanese tea-pot! let's have some tea,
A cup of the most delicious bohea!
Then plenty of sugar, and plenty of cream,
And with smiles of contentment our faces
    will beam.

FEBRUARY 25TH.

" Dolly, Dolly, tell me, dear,
    Do you like your ride ?
The go-cart's small, but so are you,
    There's room for more beside,"

FEBRUARY 26TH.

Do, pray, look at this lazy loon,
Smoking his pipe before it's noon!
Leaning his back against a rail,
While the little black dog is wagging his tail.

FEBRUARY 27TH.

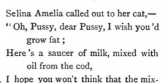

Selina Amelia called out to her cat,—
"Oh, Pussy, dear Pussy, I wish you'd
    grow fat;
Here's a saucer of milk, mixed with
    oil from the cod,
I hope you won't think that the mix-
    ture is odd."

FEBRUARY 28TH.

Shall I sing to my baby about the bright flowers?
    Shall I sing about the glad sun?
Shall I sing to my baby of long summer hours?
    Shall I sing to my sweet little one?

FEBRUARY 29TH.

A green, green tree, that stands by itself,
    A tree without very much shade ;
For its branches are cropped quite small at top,
    Until to a point it is made.

MARCH 1ST.

   Not much to be seen but a feather !
   Can it be on account of the weather ?
      We 'll suppose a fine face,
      And a great deal of grace,
   So hidden because of the weather.

MARCH 2ND.

Upright as a dart, but without much grace,
And her grandmother's bonnet quite hides her face.
I can't say much for her—now, can you ?
And I shouldn't care to say, How do you do ?

MARCH 3RD.

Now, this I call a feat of skill,
Though I should think it made him ill,—
To catch a ball, and stand like that,
Above all, when one's rather fat.

MARCH 4TH.

Miss Roundabout's dressed to go to a ball,
You'd think her so stout that she can't dance at all ;
But she is so light, she's just like a balloon,
And thinks that each dance is over too soon.

MARCH 5TH.

Little Kitty, how I love you !
I like to squeeze you to my cheek ;
Always purring, never scratching,
Always gentle, always meek.

26

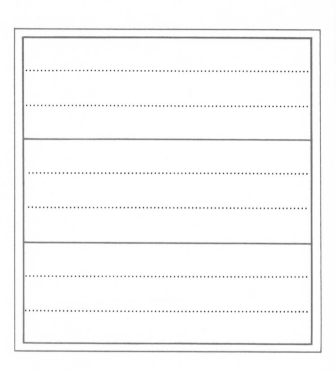

MARCH 6TH.

I was walking in the country,
    It was a little sad ;
This was the only creature near,
    The only friend I had.

MARCH 7TH.

Vain young person, who may you be,
Turning your head to look at me?
I will give you a penny, or give you a bun ;
But compliments from me, you will have none.

MARCH 8TH.

What is she looking at, up in the sky,
    Is it the moon or the sun ?
She will be dazzled, or moonstruck, perhaps,
    And then, what is to be done ?

MARCH 9TH.

Here is a round ball, give it to me,
  And I will toss it up high;
Forty times as high as the house,
  Then will it reach the sky?

MARCH 10TH.

Alack! alas! and well-a-day!
Here's never a child come out to play!
I'll tell Belinda, Clarissa, and Jane,
I never will promise to meet them again.

MARCH 11TH.

In this little wee house an old woman
    dwells,
She makes gingerbread figures, and
    lollipops sells;
The children all cheer her wherever she
    goes,
But she has a great trouble—which is a
    red nose.

28

MARCH 12TH.

" Polly, what are you looking at ?
　　What do you see out there?"
　" I see a ship sailing far, far off ;
　　And where is it going ?"—Ah, where !

MARCH 13TH.

A little Marionnette man,
　　Throwing up a ball ;
I really cannot understand
　　How he can catch at all.

MARCH 14TH.

Dear little maid !—Is she sleeping,
　Or crying her woes to the ground ?
Grief, and rest, and a little joy,—
　It is thus the world goes round.

MARCH 15TH.

Baby, baby, in the bowl,
  Have you caught an eel?
Only cotton for a line,
  To fish for Mother's reel.

MARCH 16TH.

Little Miss Sarsenet looks very glum;
Do you think that she's cross and sulky?—Hum!
It may be so, or it may not be;
Miss Sarsenet's slightly ruffled, I see.

MARCH 17TH.

Sweet are the hedges close to the stile,
  Laden with blossoms of May;
Sweet sings the river that murmurs below,
  The whole of the happy spring day.

MARCH 18TH.

Poor little wandering gipsy child,
   In rags, with feet all bare!
Come, bring some meat, and bread, and cake,
   And let her have a share.

MARCH 19TH.

This is the woman who is so fat,
There's no door she can get in at;
She has a child, so very small,
That it can scarce be seen at all.

MARCH 20TH.

Strike away! strike away!
   Make the hoop run.;
The faster it rolls,
   The greater the fun.

MARCH 21ST,

Two loving little sisters, going for a walk,
Chatter, chatter gaily, pleasantly they talk ;
What do they talk of ?   Dolls, politics, and bees ;
Both have the same views—that one plainly sees.

MARCH 22ND.

Benevolent and happy man,
    Who takes his walks abroad ;
He gives away his pence and pounds,
    And all he can afford.

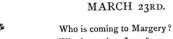

MARCH 23RD.

Who is coming to Margery ?
    Who is coming, I say ?
Some dearly loved one, who brings a plum bun,—
    That's who is coming, I say.

32

MARCH 24TH.

The wind blew hard, the wind blew strong,
And blew Lucinda fast along;
At last it blew her up in the air,
Now, has she come down, or is she still there?

MARCH 25TH.

Ah! sweet primrose, you are come,
   To tell us of the Spring;
The hedge-rows bloom, the woods are green,
   And now the birdies sing.

MARCH 26TH.

Little Patty is delighted,
    What, do you think, about?
All the flowers are shooting up,
    And the buds are out.

33

MARCH 27TH.

Poor Miss Baby, in the wind,
  Finds herself unsteady;
And she has to trot alone,
  Until Nurse is ready.

MARCH 28TH.

Lily of the Valley, very fair to see,
Sweet and dear to all I've loved, ever dear to me.
Flower, pure and fragrant, when you begin your reign,
Visions of a glad lost time will ever come again.

MARCH 29TH.

Small Billy is a coachman,
  But where—oh! where's his team?
I think they're gone to Fairyland.
  Or vanished in a dream.

MARCH 30TH.

The sails go round with a hearty swing,
    As the wild wind plays on the hill :
And the corn is crushed, and the flour ground,
    Right merrily at the mill.

MARCH 31ST.

What does the child see?—is it the moon?
Or does she look at an air balloon?
Up yet higher, ever so far,
Out there peeps the evening star.

APRIL 1ST.

Look at this boy as you pass by ;
Look, how he's laughing ! I'll tell you why :
He made an old woman an April fool ;
With vulgar boys that is the rule.

APRIL 2ND.

A pot of flowers, if you are able,
Always have upon the table ;
And a bird who 'll sweetly sing :
These things tell you of the spring.

APRIL 3RD.

Baby dear, with eyes so bright,
Staring up with all your might !
What is the sight, or what the sound,
That makes your eyes so big and round ?

APRIL 4TH.

I am walking out so early,
    To see my great-aunt Jane ;
I 'll walk a mile, and talk a while,
    And then come home again.

36

APRIL 5TH.

Tilly Toddles knocked her head
    A very hard, hard blow ;
She loudly cried, and sadly sighed
    "O dear ! it hurts me so !"

APRIL 6TH.

Running along with his flag in his hand,
    To frighten the crows away ;
We see but his back, and the crown of his hat,
    His face, p'rhaps, some other day.

APRIL 7TH.

A Normandy peasant, come out for a walk :
Could you understand if you heard her talk ?
" Bon jour, joli enfant," she would say,
Which means, " Pretty child, I wish you good day."

APRIL 8TH.

Rushes by the river-side,
   Growing proud and tall ;
The wind comes by, and makes them bow,
   Then they look quite small.

APRIL 9TH.

Baby, with the tea-cup,
   What have you got in it ?
If it is tea, give it to me ;
   Come, share it, miss, this minute.

APRIL 10TH.

Up the rope, up the rope,
   Ever so high !
Will you come down again ?
   " Yes, by-and-by."

APRIL 11TH.

Birdie, dear birdie, oh, whence do you come?
   Now say, do you bring any news?
Has mother come back from London town,
   And has she not brought me new shoes?

APRIL 12TH.

What 's in the basket, the basket?
   What is there, great or small?
Perhaps plum buns and gingerbread,
   Perhaps there's none at all.

APRIL 13TH.

Cowslips, cowslips, fresh and sweet,
   And very, very dear!
I look at you, and then go back—
   Oh, many a long, long year!

APRIL 14TH.

Mermaid, or child in a sea-shell!
Pray, little mermaid, is that where you dwell?
Blown by the wind, riding over the sea,
I'd rather it you, little mermaid, than me.

APRIL 15TH.

Little hands behind you!
    And why do you hide them, then?
Have you a ball, or nothing at all,
    But fat little fingers ten?

APRIL 16TH.

Would you like to know why I walk so fast?
    A sight I'm going to see;
It may be a ship, or it may be a shark,—
    It may, or it may not be.

APRIL 17TH.

Upon the grass, beneath the bright spring
　　sunshine,
　There sat a gentle, pensive little maid ;
The soft spring air just breathed a per-
　　fume near her,
　"I bring the kisses of the flowers,"
　　it said.

APRIL 18TH.

Who went in the fields to-day,
To gather marigolds, I say ?
Was it Belinda Abiathar Ann ?
Tell me, I pray you, if you can.

APRIL 19TH.

Dear me ! this is very odd,
　Upon the stairs to sit ;
I think she's got her night-gown on,
　And doesn't care a bit.

APRIL 20TH.

I want to see the world, you know ;
    I'm going to be a sailor :
This is my sailor suit, you see,
    Just come home from the tailor.

APRIL 21ST.

Come and look at this round plate,
Hanging alone in pomp and state.
Do you like it empty, or covered with cake?
I hope it's not always like this, for your sake.

APRIL 22ND.

"Little girl, where do you come from?
    Little girl, where do you go?"
"I come from the school in the hollow,
    Where they teach us to read and to sew."

42

APRIL 23RD.

Yes, I am fond of them ;
Now, are not you ?—
Fond of potatoes,
When they are new?

APRIL 24TH.

There was an old woman whose mind
Was fixed on a race with the wind ;
    Her friends said, " You'll find
    You'll be soon left behind ;"
But she smiled, and set off with the wind.

APRIL 25TH.

Have you got a cabbage there,
Little funny maiden fair?
"Yes, I have, I'm going to boil it,
Though the cook says I shall spoil it."

APRIL 26TH.

See, O children! now I bring
Glad sweet flowers of the spring :
May your paths with flowers be spread !
May you on them lightly tread !

APRIL 27TH.

Just an entrance, nothing more ;
    Whither, whither does it go ?—
Where glad hearts are gay and light,
    Or where they ache in silent woe ?

APRIL 28TH.

Ivy, stealthily you creep,
    Killing where you cling.
Strange ! so graceful, fair a plant,
    Should be a cruel thing.

44

APRIL 29TH.

Blowing airy bubbles light,
Watching changing colours bright :
Tommy, happy as a king,
Joyful at so small a thing.

APRIL 30TH.

Yes, they did squabble, *scratched* in their spite ;
Now they are friends again—friends again quite,
Look, how they lovingly each give a kiss ;
Now we are sure that there 's not much amiss.

MAY 1ST.

A strange-looking creature as ever was seen,
Dancing and grinning round Jack-in-the-green ;
This is an old fashion, that comes in with May,
And sad for the sweeps if the First 's a wet day.

MAY 2ND.

"Here's a nest," said a bird,
   "With my eggs in it, three;
All spotted and handsome,
   As eggs can well be."

MAY 3RD.

Tulips in the garden grow,
   Don't they make it gay?
I'm very fond of tulips,
   I'll pick one if I may.

MAY 4TH.

Little airy, fairy sprite,
   Flying in the air;
Dropping blossoms to the earth,
   Scattering flowerets fair.

46

MAY 5TH.

Is she sad, little maid,
 Or is she but sleeping?
I'd rather she dozed,
 Than made red eyes by weeping.

MAY 6TH.

When I was out a-walking,
 I met an old, old man;
What he said, and what I said,
 Now, guess it if you can.

MAY 7TH.

Come, jump off the tub—just let me see
If you can do it; now—one, two, three!
Yes, you have done it; let's merrily run
Out to the fields, and we'll have fine fun.

MAY 8TH.

This girl is dressed all spick-and-span,
    And neatly as can be ;
Her sash well tied, her mittens straight,
    She 's going out to tea.

MAY 9TH.

Wild roses grow in hedges,
    In the merry summer-time ;
I 've talked of them, and sung of them,
    And put them into rhyme.

MAY 10TH.

Watching how the daisies grow,
    In the early morning ;
At night their yellow eyes are closed,
    But open in the dawning.

MAY 11TH.

"Paddy, oh Paddy, now where do you go,
Stepping an Irish jig, dancing just so?"
"Oh, shure I'm off, then, to Dublin town,
To buy wife and children aich a new gown."

MAY 12TH.

Blossoms pink, and blossoms white,
    Flowering in May;
Sweet and bright, they bloom so fair,
    And all the world is gay.

MAY 13TH.

Such a big bonnet, a basket as big!
Is she going to market to buy a small pig?
When she comes back, it will be a fine joke,
A pig in a basket, a child in a poke.

49

MAY 14TH.

Up, up flies the shuttlecock, up with a jump;
Down on the battledore now, with a thump!
Fly away, shuttlecock, higher yet fly,
Up to the clouds that pass over the sky.

MAY 15TH.

A spirit floating through the night,
Where the stars now shed their light.
Tell us, tell us what you are?—
The Spirit of the Evening Star.

MAY 16TH.

Tulips in a pot, you see;
Phillis brought them in to me:
I thought Phillis very kind,
To pick her one I'd half a mind.

MAY 17TH.

Little Peggie has a dicky, and it is very tame ;
She loves her bird—oh, dearly ! and it loves
    her just the same ;
She gives it lots of breadcrumbs, a lump of
    sugar, too :
I wish I had a bird like that, I 'm sure, and so
    do you.

MAY 18TH.

Now, make haste, and go to school,
    Don't loiter here all day :
A girl should walk quite fast to school,
    And hurry on her way.

MAY 19TH.

Carry the baby over the fields,
    Carry her up the high hill ;
Carry her here, and carry her there,
    For baby will never be still.

51

MAY 20TH.

There was an old person who feared
The sun setting light to his beard;
So he said, " I will see, and sit under a tree,
Till the sun is too low to be feared."

MAY 21ST.

Do you want to hear the news?
I am dancing without shoes;
I can dance, and I can run,
I am up to any fun.

MAY 22ND.

A sweet, sweet sprig of lily-of-the-valley;
Who shall have it?   Little merry Sally;
She shall keep it, and wear it all day:
Lilies are found in the garden in May.

MAY 23RD.

This is Wilhelmina's back, who looks so neat and nice,
Of bread-and-butter she will take, at tea, but one
  small slice;
And when she is invited to take a little more,
She always answers softly, "I had too much before."

MAY 24TH.

Out comes a fledgling, out of his shell;
He's out in the world, but he won't see it
  well;
For off on his journey he's come but one
  mile,
And thinks he'll go back again, to rest
  awhile.

MAY 25TH.

I have a young canary,
  And he loves most to dine
On fresh green dandelion leaves,
  When they are young and fine.

MAY 26TH.

Round you go, skipping-rope, over I fly;
Which is the happiest, think, you or I?
I am the happiest, 'tis by my will
That I skip over you, or I stand still.

MAY 27TH.

Little Bobby Balancer walks upon a rail,
If he slips and has a fall—ah! then his walks
    will fail;
If he keeps his balance, and touches not the
    ground,
Then Bobby 'll reach his home again, lucky,
    safe, and sound!

MAY 28TH.

This is Joan, she is all alone,
The others have gone to the fair;
She is rather sad, for it seems too bad
That poor Joan should not also be there.

54

MAY 29TH.

This is little baby's back,
    Isn't it full of grace?
But you'd know how sweet she is,
    If you saw her face.

MAY 30TH.

What is he doing, that fat boy,
    With a bonnet on his head?
He's a lazy loon, this afternoon;
    I should send him off to bed.

MAY 31ST.

Little wild flower, that grows in the field,
    Ringing your merry bell!
What do you say in that tiny chime?—
    Pray, little flower, tell.

JUNE 1ST.

Windmills, like weathercocks, turn with the wind,
    And change, as indeed they may ;
Some little folks are exactly the same,
    Perhaps this is their birthday !

JUNE 2ND.

This weak little girl sheds a tear,
She quakes and she trembles with fear ;
But it's only a fish, though not in a dish,
So she need not display such great fear.

JUNE 3RD.

Warm little hearts, and wise little heads,
    Gentle, and loving, and kind ;
This is the way to be happy, small friends.
    And that you will very soon find.

56

JUNE 4TH.

A rose in June, a rose in June,
    That scents the summer air !
In blooming pink, I really think,
    Of flowers you are most fair.

JUNE 5TH.

Baby, baby, you look like a mouse,
Holding a bonnet as big as a house ;
Now, is it Granny's you've borrowed
    just now ?
Do you think you may keep it ?—
    will Granny allow ?

JUNE 6TH.

Blossoms, blossoms on the trees,
Swinging in the summer breeze,
Lending sweetness to the air,
To be shed on children fair.

57

JUNE 7TH.

This is Melinda, who sits all day long,
Thoughtful and pensive, composing a song;
None wish to hear it, so people say
It is not much use her composing this lay.

JUNE 8TH.

A little girl jumped for joy,
    Upon the eighth of June;
She cried, " My birthday's come at last,
    But it will go too soon."

JUNE 9TH.

Inside the window, a lady;
    Outside, a rose-tree grows:
Kind is the beautiful lady,
    Sweet is the creeping rose.

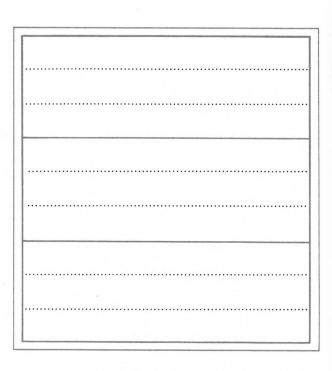

JUNE 10TH.

I'm rather idle, as you see,
   I sit upon the ground;
And all the world seems made for me,
   As it turns round and round.

JUNE 11TH.

Yes, it is sad indeed,—sad, I must say it;
That there's no croquet now, no one will
   play it.
Here stands Selina, with mallet and ball;
But no one will come and play, no one at all.

JUNE 12TH.

Ride away, ride on the branch of a tree;
How your horse canters, with action so free!
Don't ride too far, remember we're here;
Come back and tell us your travels, my dear.

59

JUNE 13TH.

Gorgeous sunflower, yellow and bright,
    Turning your face to the sun;
Glorying, basking in his glad light,
    Until his day's work is done.

JUNE 14TH.

A little girl, a little girl,
    Once went to pick some flowers;
They said, "Oh, pray go home again,
    We're sure to have some showers."

JUNE 15TH.

A carnation in our garden grows;
    How pleased we are to know it!
Our gardener said we should have one,
    He said, "I'm going to sow it."

JUNE 16TH.

A pretty tree, a shady tree,
  Just casts its shadow round;
And we can go and sit beneath,
  If we don't mind the ground.

JUNE 17TH.

Janet plays at ball all day,
  Through the hot, hot weather;
Her ball is small, but very hard,
  Because it's made of leather.

JUNE 18TH.

Tiger-lily, tall and straight,
  How handsomely you grow!
Your spotted leaves, and yellow tongues—
  But stop!—you're vain, I know.

JUNE 19TH.

Margery has a new skipping-rope,
    Margery skips all the day :
Bobby and Bill hate the skipping,
    For Margery with them won't play.

JUNE 20TH.

Little girl leaning against the stile,
    Are you resting yourself awhile ?
Do you think—how sweet is the summer day,
    When all the world seems made for play ?

JUNE 21ST.

Little flower of the field,
    To me you tell a tale,
Of blooms upon the hill-side,
    Of blossoms in the vale.

JUNE 22ND.

This girl is walking to London town,
　　Her luncheon in her basket ;
She's walking, walking up and down,
　　Her way—she'll have to ask it.

JUNE 23RD.

Dear moon-daisies, I love you ;
　　Old friends, that I know so well ;
Glad scenes come back when I see you,
　　And sad thoughts that I dare not tell.

JUNE 24TH.

Poppy, poppy, flaunting red,
　　In the meadow green ;
You are so bold, you stare about,
　　And you are always seen.

JUNE 25TH.

Against a post leant Tabitha,
    Her fan within her hand;
She looked about, did Tabitha,
    And she surveyed the land.

JUNE 26TH.

These are the two Miss Minevers,
    So good, so very good!
They each do what the other likes,
    As sisters always should.

JUNE 27TH.

I am a mountain daffodil,
    My colour it is yellow;
I think the whole world must agree,
    I am a handsome fellow.

JUNE 28TH.

This is a house, it's very straight,
　　And also rather tall;
And lovers of the picturesque
　　Don't like this house at all.

JUNE 29TH.

This flower grows within my garden,
　　Perhaps you have the same;
If that's the case, of course you know it,
　　Pray, therefore, tell its name.

JUNE 30TH.

There was a young person whose passion
Was always to dress in the fashion;
　　That she did not succeed,
　　To tell there's no need,
For you see that she's not in the fashion.

65

JULY 1ST.

There she goes with her pitchfork,
　　To turn about the hay,
To toss it up, and spread it out,
　　On this hot summer day.

JULY 2ND.

This is a beautiful Iris,
　　Soft purple is its hue
I think it a grand-looking flower,
　　Now tell me, do not you?

JULY 3RD.

The sweetest, freshest, pinkest rose!
　　The rose-tree in our garden grows;
It is sweet to sight and smell;
　　Indeed, we love that rose-tree well.

JULY 4TH.

I lie beside the running stream,
And watch the clouds, and rest, and dream;
A jug with water by me stands,
Which I have filled with my own hands.

JULY 5TH.

Sitting on the wall!
It is not safe at all.
Come, come, get down, I say;
You can't sit there all day.

JULY 6TH.

How I love the field flowers,
  Blooming bright and gay!
How I love the green, green fields,
  To wander there all day!

JULY 7TH.

Most certainly I hardly know
    If she has doll or baby;
Perhaps you know, you are so wise,
    And think me but a gaby.

JULY 8TH.

That girl has got a large round hat,
    Perhaps a round red face;
We cannot judge how this may be,
    But only of her grace.

JULY 9TH.

Currants black, and currants red,
    Let's have some in a pie,
With sugar and delicious cream,—
    We 'll have some by-and-by.

JULY 10TH.

Letty and Etty walked hand in hand,
Pleasantly, quietly through the broad land ;
Letty and Etty said, " Are we not good ?
We walk and we talk just as little girls should."

JULY 11TH.

Lily, lily, white and tall,
    You are wondrous fair ;
I bid you welcome to this book,
    I 'm glad you 're standing there.

JULY 12TH.

Little Phillipina stands to watch the sun,
Thinks she'll stand and watch it till its work is done ;
Little Phillipina, you must watch all day,
For the sun will shine till night, and then he'll go away.

JULY 13TH.

I look at this, and here is seen
A little sprig of creeping bean;
I like to eat them, I like them growing,
I like them in this picture showing.

JULY 14TH.

Do you like gooseberries? I can't say I do;
Perhaps you like currants, and raspberries too.
I wish you could come to our country home,
How much in the garden you would like to roam!

JULY 15TH.

To market they go, on St. Swithin's day,
They've something to sell, and something to pay;
They've one big umbrella to keep off the rain,
Which comes, on that Saint's day, again and again.

JULY 16TH.

It's very sad to stand alone,
    Upon a summer's day,
And long to see some chubby child,
    To have a game at play.

JULY 17TH.

A bramble once looked over a rail,
  "We shall have some rain," she said;
"Well, it's time that the grass should have a drink,
    And it's time that the dust was laid."

JULY 18TH.

White and blue convolvulus!
    At four it goes to bed,
With bell closed tight with all its might,
    Perhaps you've heard it said?

71

JULY 19TH.

This funny old woman takes care of her dog,
    Her sun-shade protects her and it;
"It's the dog-days, you know, and think, if poor Flo
    "Went mad," said she, "and then bit!"

JULY 20TH.

The shuttlecock up in the air has flown,
Oh, where, and oh, where is it gone?
Alack and alack! will it never come back?
The battledore's left all forlorn.

JULY 21ST.

This is Johnny, who says, "I've heard the hen cackle,
    I'm sure that some eggs she has laid;
I'll go to the hen-house, and fill up my basket—
    That is, if I don't feel afraid."

JULY 22ND.

When we have the warm, warm sunshine,
    That is when the flowers grow ;
In the garden, by the footpath,
    Stand the flowers in a row.

JULY 23RD.

Up the post the rose-tree twines,
    With its blossoms sweet and fair ;
To its neighbour lends a grace—
    To the post, so plain and bare.

JULY 24TH.

Hurrah, hurrah, for harvest-time !
    Hurrah for the grain our land yields !
Hurrah, hurrah, for the harvest-home,
    For the yellow sheaves in the fields !

JULY 25TH.

As I went out to take the air,
　　I met two maidens small ;
I greeted them politely,
　　But they answered not at all.

JULY 26TH.

A maiden went a-gleaning,
　　Upon a summer's day ;
She gleaned and gleaned a goodly sheaf,
　　Then went upon her way.

JULY 27TH.

Daffodils grow in the meadows,
　　Scenting the summer air :
Daffodils out in the garden,—
　　I 'm glad I have them there.

JULY 28TH.

When I have no flowers, I love the leaves so green;
And the dainty leaf of a creeping plant is prettiest
     to be seen;
And if I can have flowers, with them I leaves
     entwine,
So round the clustering blossoms lie the leaves of
     the creeping vine.

JULY 29TH.

This girl has got the baby, I hope she will take care;
I think she might forget it—forget that it is there.
She wears so large a bonnet, that she really cannot see;
And she might drop the baby, and then how sad
     t'would be!

JULY 30TH.

"My greatest delight," said Timothy White,
    " Is to swing by my arms all day;
To me people call, 'Pray come down, you
     will fall;'
    But I laugh, and continue my play."

JULY 31ST.

Flowers yellow, leaves all green,
Here's a puffy ball between;
The children blow those balls away,
"They're clocks, and tell the time," they say.

AUGUST 1ST.

Here's a girl, she has a basket,
What is in it—do you ask it?
I heard a miow! it is a cat!
Now, children, what do you think of that?

AUGUST 2ND.

A small, small branch of a very large tree;
Pray, little folks, say what it may be?
It is shady and grand, and grows in our land,
And it is reckoned a very fine tree.

AUGUST 3RD.

Tommy Thumbkin rides a barrel,—
    Where does his journey lead ?
To No-where Town, which is miles away,
    He rides on his stalwart steed.

AUGUST 4TH.

A pot of flowers—oh, how sweet
Flowers always are a treat ;
In a garden or a pot,
We all love flowers—do we not ?

AUGUST 5TH.

This tree grows in a garden,
    Where merry children run ;
They like this funny little tree,
    It shelters them from sun.

AUGUST 6TH.

This lady has come to pay a call,
    To have a little chat ;
She talks of the weather, she talks of the news,
    She talks of this and of that.

AUGUST 7TH.

Poor croquet balls ! quite idle,
    They've got no work to do ;
Just like frozen-out gardeners,
    That in winter trouble you.

AUGUST 8TH.

How doth the greedy little bee
    Take honey to his hive ;
And sting, and buzz, and much annoy,
    And to be foremost strive.

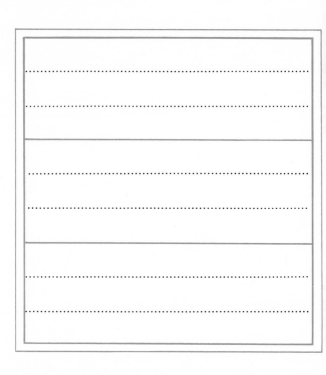

AUGUST 9TH.

What does little Johnny see?—
    A waggon with horses four ;
Each horse has a bell, and it jingles well,
    But Johnny wishes for more.

AUGUST 10TH.

Plums, plums, purple plums !
    Do you like them in a tart ?
I like to pick them from the tree,
    And eat them, for my part.

AUGUST 11TH.

Flowers now are getting scarce,
    I regret to say ;
How very, very sad 'twill be,
    When all are gone away !

AUGUST 12TH.

Upon a gate, beside a moor,
This boy sits quiet as a mouse ;
He hears the sportsmen shooting near,
They're killing, killing little grouse.

AUGUST 13TH.

What is this boy staring at ?
  I dare say you wonder too ;
Try as I may, I cannot say,
  But it must be something new.

AUGUST 14TH.

A player at croquet at last,
So it's not quite a thing of the past ;
This girl is quite ready, with mallet in hand,
So I hope she won't have alone long to stand.

AUGUST 15TH.

This damsel seems extremely proud,
    Her nose so high in air ;
I really don't think much of her,
    Such pride I cannot bear.

AUGUST 16TH.

What have you there, you dear little girl ?
    What have you there, now tell ?
Are they good, good things, you will have for tea ;
    Or things that you want to sell ?

AUGUST 17TH.

Out in the garden Miss Peachblossom ran,
A hat on her head, in her hand a great fan ;
" I smell the sweet flowers—a bird past me flies ;
Good-bye, pretty garden !" and back she then hies.

AUGUST 18TH.

Darling baby, as you look
Straight at me from out this book;
How I wish that I could take you,
And a real live baby make you!

AUGUST 19TH.

A very small man, with cocked hat so gay,
Remarkably active, he runs fast away;
A neat little figure, compact, and so brave,
As in triumph he lifts up his banner to wave.

AUGUST 20TH.

An Italian peasant, by a well;
Who she is I cannot tell;
She wears a very curious cap,
Awkward, if she took a nap.

AUGUST 21ST.

A storm in a tea-pot, I declare !
    Do tell me what's the matter !
This little person's quite put out,
    That's why there s such a clatter.

AUGUST 22ND.

A train goes by, and Tommy runs,
    And holds a flag quite high ;
It is such fun, small Tommy thinks,
    To see a train go by.

AUGUST 23RD.

This girl is waiting for somebody,
    For whom is she waiting, I say?
I think it's for the pedlar,
    Who often comes this way.

AUGUST 24TH.

Peter is running, oh, running!
  And why does he run so fast?
He teased an old hen, who flew at him then,
  And he thinks she will catch him at last.

AUGUST 25TH.

Eliza Jane she goes to market,
  Upon a market-day;
You'd like to know why it is so?
  Well, really, I can't say.

AUGUST 26TH.

An old person once said, " I will try,
A very large bonnet to buy;
  The neighbours will see,
  And all envy me
This very large bonnet I buy."

84

AUGUST 27TH.

Little Hodge-Podge, he sat on a stile,
He thought that he would rest awhile;
He dozed, and dozed, and fell asleep,
And then fell in the ditch so deep.

AUGUST 28TH.

Now Dolly, dear Dolly, I'll put you to bed;
I have a big apron, a cap on my head;
You know I'm Nurse Crabbed, and very severe;
So take care you are good—now mind that,
  Dolly dear.

AUGUST 29TH.

The two twin Master Twinklebys
  Are good and quiet boys;
They neither tear their sister's hair,
  Nor do they cry for toys.

AUGUST 30TH.

What a big umbrella ! and oh, what a hat !
  What a curious person is he !
I've travelled for many and many a mile,
  Yet the like of him never did see.

AUGUST 31ST.

Grapes, grapes ! don't you like them ?
  Purple, large, and sweet !
Little children, come and pick them,
  Come, and let us eat.

SEPTEMBER 1ST.

There was an old person who heard
Some shots fired near, at a bird ;
Said he, " Now I remember,
'Tis the first of September ;
But there flies the fortunate bird."

86

SEPTEMBER 2ND.

Here there stands a little form,
    So very lightly clad,
I really fear she will be cold,
    And it seems quite too bad.

SEPTEMBER 3RD.

He's watching a balloon,
    That went up this afternoon;
It's gone so very high, right into the blue sky,
    But it's sure to come down soon.

SEPTEMBER 4TH.

This is dejected Ann,
Look at her while you can;
She will not skip, and I'm really fearful
She'll melt away, she is so tearful.

SEPTEMBER 5TH.

Baby ran to meet me, she had a sash all blue,
    A bran-new gown,
      Just come from town,
    A cap so crisp and new.

SEPTEMBER 6TH.

A goodly melon,
    Colours green and yellow ;
Flavour most delicious,
    Sweet and very mellow !

SEPTEMBER 7TH.

Going to school in the morning,
    With her bag by her side, and her slate ;
She stands and stares at the passers-by,
    I'm sure that she will be late.

SEPTEMBER 8TH.

Here I am, with mallet and ball,—
  Who is going to play?
It is no use for me to stand
  And wait for you all day.

SEPTEMBER 9TH.

Apples, rosy-cheeked apples!
  Clustering on the tree;
I'd give you one, or give you two,
  If they belonged to me.

SEPTEMBER 10TH.

Thomasina looks afar,
  She sees a train go by;
"I declare that this minute I wish I was
    in it,"
  Thomasina said, with a sigh.

SEPTEMBER 11TH.

Yes, see her standing there,
  Watering flowers;
She loves her garden,
  And works there for hours.

SEPTEMBER 12TH.

Lawn-tennis this girl thinks a very fine game;
Perhaps, little friends, you all think the same;
You have to be active, and you get very hot,
And the boys are the best at it,—now, are they not?

SEPTEMBER 13TH.

Just a branch with apples,
  Tinted red and green;
The prettiest branch with apples
  That I have ever seen.

SEPTEMBER 14TH.

A girl sat on a wall one day,
She was tired, and would not play;
I called, "You'll fall," from the foot of the hill,
But she paid no heed, and sat there still.

SEPTEMBER 15TH.

There she stands at the garden gate,
But she has come so very late;
The flowers are going, the leaves now fall,
T'were better, perhaps, if she came not at all.

SEPTEMBER 16TH.

A sweet, fair maiden rested on the plain;
Rested, and went, and never came again;
Oh! little maid, now dreary is the spot,
Oh! little maid, 'tis there, but you are not.

SEPTEMBER 17TH.

Two brave stacks of famous hay,
Well stacked upon a summer day;
The crows think, as they homeward fly,
Some hay will keep our nests quite dry.

SEPTEMBER 18TH.

Oh, dear me, what a flurry !
You seem in a desperate hurry;
  You keep up such a pace,
  Are you running a race,
That you fly along in a scurry?

SEPTEMBER 19TH.

Gaily dancing, tripping along,
Jumping high, and singing a song;
In your hair you've put a rose,—
I think you rather want some clothes.

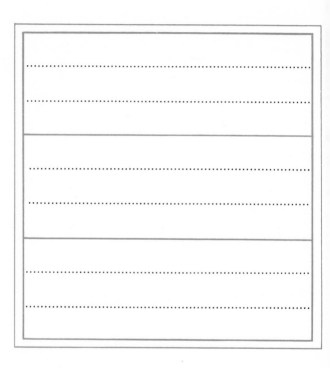

SEPTEMBER 20TH.

One large apple! is it for me?
Who has picked it off the tree?
We'll have it peeled, and put in a pie,
And then we'll eat it, you and I.

SEPTEMBER 21ST.

I should think it very hard,
  And also rather sad,
To dance alone, with so much grace,—
  Indeed, it is too bad.

SEPTEMBER 22ND.

Polly has got a new Bow-wow,
  Polly is merry and gay;
Polly thinks the whole world bright,
  And this the happiest day.

SEPTEMBER 23RD.

Digging, digging on the sands,
  With a bran-new spade;
Piling up the sand so high,
  Until a castle's made.

SEPTEMBER 24TH.

He's trying to catch a great big fish,
And then he'll put it in a dish;
He and his wife on it will sup,
Perhaps they'll eat the monster up.

SEPTEMBER 25TH.

Reading a book with a steadfast look,
  So studiously inclined;
To run away with child and book,
  I think I've half a mind.

SEPTEMBER 26TH.

Johnny aud Julia, two good little things,
    Sat on the ground together;
They talked of the birds, and talked of
      the trees,
    Enjoying the sunshiny weather.

SEPTEMBER 27TH.

A very big apple, a very large pear—
A nice dessert for us to share;
Let us divide them both in two,
And take two halves, both I and you.

SEPTEMBER 28TH.

Run, run, Elizabeth, run very fast!
If you don't catch it, the ball will go past;
Run, run, Elizabeth! see, it will fall!
Make haste, or else you won't catch it at all.

SEPTEMBER 29TH.

A large dish of grapes !
    Come, come, let us eat ;
I think, for you little ones
    This is a treat,

SEPTEMBER 30TH.

Who has been in the woods to-day ?
    Who has been there a-nutting ?
With long-hooked sticks, and baskets too ;
    The branches they've been cutting.

OCTOBER 1ST.

This is the day that the pheasants dread,
For the poor little things are shot through the
            head ;
This little boy will help covers to beat,
And then there'll be plenty of pheasants to eat.

OCTOBER 2ND.

This boy is going to sail his boat,
   In a certain pond so round;
The pond is in Kensington Gardens,—
   You know it, I'll be bound.

OCTOBER 3RD.

Oh, here we are in the country!
   Look at this bowl of cream!
And, you will see, five-o'clock tea
   Delightful now will seem.

OCTOBER 4TH.

Out of the sweet, sweet flowers
   This funny goblin sprang;
And all the roses shook their heads,
   And all the blue-bells rang.

OCTOBER 5TH.

A girl went walking by herself,
　　The wind was rather high;
" Blow hard, old wind !" this bold girl cried,
　　" I do not care, not I."

OCTOBER 6TH.

Phœbe has a new battledore,
　　And a new shuttlecock too :
" I shall send you flying, shuttlecock,"
　　Said Phœbe, " that's what I'll do."

OCTOBER 7TH.

There has been rain, on the ground is dirt,
　　And so Cecilia holds up her skirt;
She holds her skirt, you see, quite high,
　　To keep it clean, and also dry.

98

OCTOBER 8TH.

A Bishop's-thumb, I do declare!—
That is the name of this queer pear;
Were I a Bishop, I should fidget,
To have so oddly-shaped a digit.

OCTOBER 9TH.

"What are you looking at, Sally?" said she,
   "What do you see round there?"
"I see an old woman who rides a cock-horse,
   And a maiden with golden hair."

OCTOBER 10TH.

Come and play at cricket now,
   Come along, you boys;
Mind how you come, and quickly come,
   And do not make a noise.

OCTOBER 11TH.

What fun children have,
    When the horse-chesnuts come!
They peel them, and string them,—
    Now go and get some.

OCTOBER 12TH.

"Where are you going this morning?
Where are you going this morning?"
"I hear the Queen is to be seen,
And I'm going to see her this morning."

OCTOBER 13TH.

Here's a pear,—
Not here, but there;
I mean, in the book,
If you will but look.

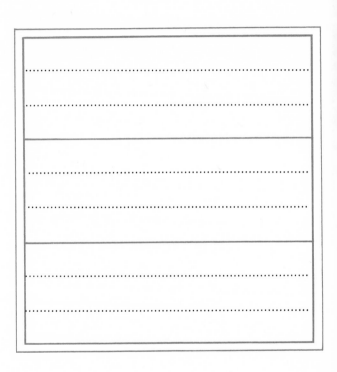

OCTOBER 14TH.

What is this boy fishing for?
    What does he hope to get?
He hopes to get a very fine fish.
    But I think he will get wet.

OCTOBER 15TH.

Why does she cry, this dear little trot?
    And why does she suck her thumb?
It cannot be sweet—it is horrid to eat;
    So, instead, let us give her a plum.

OCTOBER 16TH.

Tabitha has a hoop to bowl,
    And Tabitha's very glad;
Tabitha had no hoop one day,
    Then Tabitha was sad.

OCTOBER 17TH.

This boy now sees a large, large ship,
    That's sailing out to sea;
His heart is sore, for one he loves
    Must in that large ship be.

OCTOBER 18TH.

John and Joan go up to town,
    London town to view;
" The streets are gold, so we are told;
    We'll see, both I and you."

OCTOBER 19TH.

" I've a nice new bonnet," an old dame said,
    " It shelters me well, I know;
Some people think it a trifle large,
    And perhaps it may be so."

OCTOBER 20TH.

Janet didn't know her lesson,
    Janet said it badly;
Janet was rebuked severely,
    Janet took it sadly.

OCTOBER 21ST.

"Hip, hip, hurrah!" cried Jonathan Green,
  "The Queen will soon pass by;
I don't care a mite for all the grand sight,
  But to see the Queen I'll try."

OCTOBER 22ND.

"Ride, little brother, ride on my back;
  Where shall we go to now?
Up to the sty, to see the pig,
  To the meadow to see the cow?"

OCTOBER 23RD.

Sammy has a little line,
    His mother has a dish,
On which small Sammy trusts that he
    May shortly place a fish,

OCTOBER 24TH.

Little fairy in a shell, sailing o'er the sea!
Whither are you coming?—perhaps to visit me.
Where, then, do you come from, o'er the stormy
    main?
Little fairy, how I trust you'll get back safe again!

OCTOBER 25TH.

Little Polly has an old dolly,
    She loves it—oh, so dearly!
She cannot see how ugly it be,
    Though we can, very clearly.

104

OCTOBER 26TH.

Sweet little girl, now where do you look?
  Do tell me what it can be.
" I'm looking and longing for my Mamma,
  And she is across the sea."

OCTOBER 27TH.

Turnips, if done in this way,
Will cure a cold, so they say:
Cut the turnips into slices, put them in a pan,
A little water, some brown sugar, and—eat
    them, if you can.

OCTOBER 28TH.

Now listen, while I tell you
    About this little maid,
Who went out with her Mamma,—
    But now it all is said.

OCTOBER 29TH.

Little Baby's dressed, and waits—
　　Dressed to go a-tata;
Who do you think he's going with?
　　He's going out with Papa.

OCTOBER 30TH.

The leaves are turning brown and dry,
They fall all round as we pass by;
The country looks all cold and drear,
No flowers, no fruit, no birds are here.

OCTOBER 31ST.

Here's a jar of apples,
　　And here we have a pan:
'Tis Allhallow E'en,
And now, I ween,
　　You've all the fun you can.

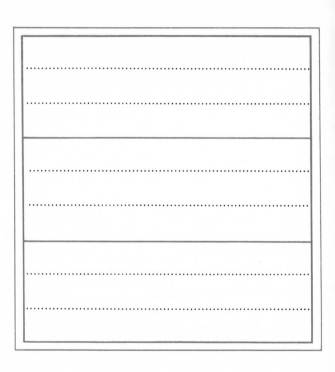

NOVEMBER 1ST.

This is little Hodge we see,
Sitting down and having tea;
Let us hope the tea is hot,
For sure it is, the weather's not.

NOVEMBER 2ND.

Penelope goes to see her aunt,
  And sits demure and prim;
For Auntie is an ancient maid,
  Both angular and slim.

NOVEMBER 3RD.

Here is a pair of pears!
  Cissy and you are a pair;
Let us divide the pair of pears
  Between the other pair.

107

NOVEMBER 4TH.

Darling little Lily has this Birthday Book,
Into it the little child casts many and many a look;
And I know she likes it—so, I hope, do you;
It's made to please the children—that I always try to do.

NOVEMBER 5TH.

Remember, my friends, 'tis the fifth of November;
  This is a fine guy, is he not?
When such creatures we see, no reason there'll be,
  Why Guy Fawkes' Day should e'er be forgot.

NOVEMBER 6TH.

I stand upon the shore
I hear the great waves roar;
I see the great ships tost,
I pray that none be lost.

108

NOVEMBER 7TH.

What can I give you, Ma'am, to-day?
  Sausage, ham, or mutton-pie,
Beef, or tongue, or chickens fine?
  To please your taste, Ma'am, I will try.

NOVEMBER 8TH.

Leafless trees are standing bare,
  Against the cold autumnal sky;
Alas, for the buds and blossoms gone!
  Alas, for the summer past! we sigh.

NOVEMBER 9TH.

What is Harry looking at,
  Why does he stand and stare?
He sees a grand sight, that gives him delight,
  The Lord Mayor's Procession is there!

NOVEMBER 10TH.

You see, little Anna has got a large dish
    Of apples so rosy and fair ;
She is coming this way, so I very much hope
    She'll invite all her friends here to share.

NOVEMBER 11TH.

    Here's a little milkmaid,
        Very welcome, too ;
    Give us some nice milk to drink,
        Little milkmaid, do !

NOVEMBER 12TH.

This girl has just come back from school,
    She sits and rests awhile ;
She's rather tired now, you know,
    For she's walked many a mile.

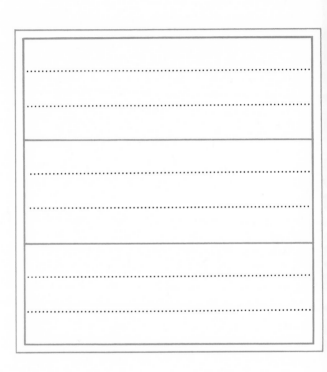

NOVEMBER 13TH.

"I must go to the stables,
    I must hie to the barn;
I must look to the horses,
    And see they come to no harm."

NOVEMBER 14TH.

"Oh, buy my oranges! buy, I pray!
    I'm very—very poor;
You're warm and happy in your homes,
    I stand cold at the door."

NOVEMBER 15TH.

A very old goblin lives in this tower,
    He eats nothing but mustard and batter;
And why should he choose such very odd fare?
    I will tell you—he's mad as a hatter.

NOVEMBER 16TH.

She walked along, with her bonnet so big,
    And she carried her bag by her side;
"Ho, ho! there's a fine old girl, to be sure!"
    The rude street-boys then cried.

NOVEMBER 17TH.

Polly Perkins carries a pan,
What is in it? guess, if you can;
Perhaps it's some water to wash her face,
But I can't say she carries the pan with much grace.

NOVEMBER 18TH.

This is Miss Jessie, she looks rather prim,
With her nice great-coat and her hat so trim;
Where is she going, this cold day?
I do not know, so cannot say.

NOVEMBER 19TH.

How cold she must be, that poor little mite !
   Look at her little bare arm ;
I hope that Jack Frost won't give her a bite,
   That the weather will not do her harm.

NOVEMBER 20TH.

Strike the tree, woodman,
   Strike, strike away !
Strike, strike the grand old tree,
   Strike while you may !

NOVEMBER 21ST.

A lady went a-walking,
   She was so fair, so fair !
Alas ! it is a picture,
   She is not really there.

NOVEMBER 22ND.

Jack was such a clever boy!
  "I like to work," he said;
You see, he now goes off to school,
  To cram his busy head.

NOVEMBER 23RD.

What do you think of her?
  I think she's plain;
If you ask me once more,
  I shall say so again.

NOVEMBER 24TH.

Here's a little woman,
  Carrying a large tray;
Where does she come from?
  Guess it now you may.

NOVEMBER 25TH.

Little folks, here's an empty chair,
See now how many of you it can bear;
Do you think two, do you think three?
I think that depends on how heavy you be.

NOVEMBER 26TH.

A very long dress, and a queer frilled cap,
   She carries a basket, too;
I've no more to say,
Perhaps, though, you may:
   I am not so clever as you.

NOVEMBER 27TH.

A brigand's hat! well, what of that,
   If there's no head within?
To take off one without the other,
   I really call a sin.

NOVEMBER 28TH.

This is Obadiah,
  Who walks on the sands,
And carries a pail
  In his little hands.

NOVEMBER 29TH.

Have pity, children, on the poor !
  Their days are full of woe ;
They have few clothes, so little food,
  No home where they can go.

NOVEMBER 30TH.

There was an old man who was bent,
And over his stick he oft leant ;
  He said, " But for my sticks,
  I should be in a fix,
For I really am terribly bent."

116

DECEMBER 1ST.

This is a screen, a hand-screen,
    A screen that came from China!
And who do you think, now, gave it me?
    Why, it was cousin Dinah.

DECEMBER 2ND.

A tiny house, a nice wee house,
    A house that just suits me;
And when we're really settled there,
    I hope you'll come and see.

DECEMBER 3RD.

Sweep, sweep, old woman,
    Sweep, sweep away;
Sweep all the dust and dirt,
    Fast as you may.

DECEMBER 4TH.

This is Phil, who says he's ill,
　　And cannot go to school ;
He's running just the other way :
　　He will grow up a fool.

DECEMBER 5TH.

On a cold, cold day in December,
　　Delightful it is, to be sure,
To sit in front of the fire ;
　　But take care there's no draught
　　　　from the door.

DECEMBER 6TH.

This is Angelina, going for a walk,
She can smile so pleasantly, and so nicely talk ;
She is indeed so sweet a child, that like her there are few
She is a dear good little girl, and so, perhaps, are you.

DECEMBER 7TH.

Here's a handsome cup, I wonder what is in it?
Give a guess now, children, say what you think,
    this minute ;
Lily says it's chocolate, Johnny says it's tea ;
Now, children, what do you say ?   Please to tell
    it me.

DECEMBER 8TH.

Certainly she's tall and slight,
Certainly a weight quite light ;
Certainly I don't admire
This tall, straight dame, or her attire.

DECEMBER 9TH.

Poor little beggar-girl, out in the cold !
Show pity, all you who have silver and gold ;
Give from your plenty all you can spare,
With the poor and the wretched be willing to share.

DECEMBER 10TH.

A broom in his hand, a mop on his head,
    A little merry boy;
Few playthings he has, so he takes the broom,
    To serve him for a toy.

DECEMBER 11TH.

This is good Mr. Longnose,
    For his learning famed, and sense;
P'rhaps the knowledge he has gained
    Has made his nose immense.

DECEMBER 12TH.

See what a poor little ragged lad!
It really makes me very sad
To see a boy in such a state;
Now think, how very hard his fate.

120

DECEMBER 13TH.

Phœbe sits upon a stool,
    Of legs it has but three;
It may be big enough for her,
    But not for you or me.

DECEMBER 14TH.

Here we are on a cold, cold night,
Rolled up warm, so nice and tight;
Going off to see a play,
At the close of a winter's day.

DECEMBER 15TH.

What do you want now, Billy?
What do you want, I say?
    "I've been a good boy,
      So I want a toy,
And a plum-bun this day."

DECEMBER 16TH.

Here's a merry lad, I ween,
Happy he, as King or Queen;
Glad is he to take your penny,
Still he smiles if you've not any.

DECEMBER 17TH.

A coachman ready for the road,
   Wrapped up from chin to toes;
He has something tragic on his mind,
   Which troubles ere he goes.

DECEMBER 18TH.

I think we come upon a fancy ball,
Or else I cannot make him out at all;
His curious hat, with large and drooping feather,
His dress, unsuited to the time or weather.

122

DECEMBER 19TH.

A Dresden china figure this,
   How pretty, children—look!
We really find some curious things
   Within this Birthday Book.

DECEMBER 20TH.

And where do you come from, with shillalagh in your
      hand?
"Shure, and plase yer honor, I come from Paddyland,
Auld Ireland, the island of praties and milk;
And shure, blarney, too—ain't our tongues soft as silk?"

DECEMBER 21ST.

What archer is this? Why, bold Robin Hood;
He has left all his men, and come out of the wood;
He thought you would like to handle the bow,
So the best way to do so he thought he would show,

DECEMBER 22ND.

This is Hang-me-up-hi, the mandarin,
As grand a Chinese as ever was seen;
Look at his pigtail, look at his toes,
And all his very magnificent clothes.

DECEMBER 23RD.

Here's another little fellow,
In fancy dress, you see;
A little cavalier, I think,
That he must really be.

DECEMBER 24TH.

Christmas Eve! Now, all you merry children,
Hang up your stockings, and sink to happy rest;
Then gliding through the room the Christ-child passes,
And breathing near the sleepers, leaves them blest.

DECEMBER 25TH.

Christmas ! Hear the joy-bells ringing,
Glad hymns in the churches singing ;
Of His mercy, of His power,
And the gifts good angels shower !

DECEMBER 26TH.

Why does she wear a steeple stuck upon her head ?
This is a mediæval dress, so I've heard it said ;
Why has she got a battledore and shuttlecock in
       hand ?
To tell the truth, this lady I cannot understand.

DECEMBER 27TH.

A person once said, " I will run ;
You can have no idea of the fun
    Of running so fast
    That you drop down at last,
And feel that you're utterly done."

DECEMBER 28TH.

Little Bopeep, I declare,
　　With little hat and crook !
How nice to find so old a friend
　　Within the Birthday Book.

DECEMBER 29TH.

Yes, I was sure of it, sure as could be,
And yet he would not listen to me;
He kicked his legs, and he made them sore,
With those ridiculous spurs he wore !

DECEMBER 30TH.

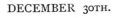

This looks to me like a dreadful robber;
　　Is it he who left the " Babes in the Wood,"
To perish sadly with cold and hunger,
　　Covered with leaves by the dickies good?

DECEMBER 31ST.

This old woman takes a fly,
To sweep the cobwebs off the sky.
She says, " As I'm going up so high,
I wish the old year, and you all, Good-bye."